WATERMEAD P
Journeys through

# HOLY WEEK & EASTER
## *Suppers ✠ Cross ✠ Resurrection*

Fr John Daley IC

Watermead Publishing Limited

## WATERMEAD PATHWAYS
*Journeys through the Gospel*
Book Seven **'Easter & Holy Week: Suppers ✠ Cross ✠ Resurrection'**

### ISBN 978-1-907721-08-3

© John Daley *(Individual Texts)*

© 2022 Alison Kennedy *("Easter & Holy Week" Presentation)*

All rights reserved on all publications.
No part of this publication may be reproduced or transmitted in any form or by any means, electronic or mechanical, including photocopying, recording or any information storage and retrieval system now known to be invented, without permission in writing from the publishers.

First Published 19th March 2022 by
Watermead Publishing Limited,
Watermead Centre, St Joseph's, 12 Goodwood Road, Leicester LE5 6SG
Telephone 0116 2207881

© Images detailed below are copyright of Watermead Publishing Apostolate
Cover Picture *"At the Foot of the Cross"* (Graphic Collage) Alison Kennedy
Station drawings by David Warner (page 1), taken from the tapestry Stations of the Cross at St Theresa's Church, Birstall, Leicestershire. Original tapestry designs by Vanessa Esposito
*Emmaus* (page 15) David Kennedy : *Tomb* (page 22) by Bernadette Mulligan Cant
*Christ is Risen* (Page 31) by Sheila Jackson

© Watermead "Verba" Collections 18 (page 20)
Various quotations adapted from scripture and the prayer

Editing, design, and typesetting by Alison Kennedy
with grateful thanks to our proof readers Barbara and Catherine

Watermead Publishing Apostolate
**www.watermead-apostolate.co.uk**

### Watermead Pathways Series
Book One *"FaithGift"* published April 2010
Book Two *"LoveGift"* published March 2011
Book Three *"ChristGift"* published December 2013
Book Four *"Rome - Just around the Corner"* published December 2020
Book Five *"Saints & Holy Souls"* published November 2021
Book Six *"Together with God in Healing and Hope"* published February 2022

### Other Publications from the Watermead Apostolate
*"Words of Prayer and Encouragement"* (published by Watermead Publishing Ltd)
*"Words of Prayer and Reflection"* (published by Catholic Printing Company of Farnworth)
*"Voices of the Gospels"* by Colleen Wethered (published by Catholic Printing Company of Farnworth)
*"Tom, an English Irishman"* by T.P. Concannon (published by Watermead Publishing Ltd)
*"O Lord, Hear my Prayer"* (published by Watermead Publishing Ltd)
*"Getting to Know the Bible"* (published by Redemptorist Publications)
*"The Parables of Jesus - the Musical"* (published by Watermead Publishing Ltd)
*"Knocking on Heaven's Door"* by Don Maclean (published by Watermead Publishing Ltd)

# CONTENTS

The Stations of the Cross ............................................. 1

Palm Sunday ................................................................. 2

Date of the Last Supper .............................................. 4

Standing near the Cross .............................................. 6

Mary of Clopas ............................................................. 8

The Shroud and Holy Saturday Night ....................... 10

The Four Resurrection Stories .................................. 12

Gospel Moments: The Breaking of Bread ............... 14

The Twelve, or so, Apostles ...................................... 16

The Evangelists ........................................................... 17

Like that? ..................................................................... 18

Wood's Secrets ........................................................... 20

Holy Week and Easter: Telling the Story ................ 21

Christ's Farewell (a hymn) ........................................ 25

A Gospel Quiz ............................................................. 28

Quiz Answers .............................................................. 30

# *Before you Read . . . .*

*There is one Gospel – the Good News of Jesus Christ,
but we know the Gospel in four different tellings
"according to Matthew, Mark, Luke, John".
In this little book the names of the four evangelists serve
as the full reference title, and "according to . . ." is omitted.*

*You will understand that certain details are repeated
in some of the chapters to help the story move smoothly,
rather than have the need to refer to other pages.*

*You will notice that sometimes the book reads as
'now' ("Jesus enters"), sometimes as 'past' ("Jesus entered").
This reflects the way people vary in the ways
of telling their own stories.*

# THE STATIONS OF THE CROSS

✠

A Lenten Journey

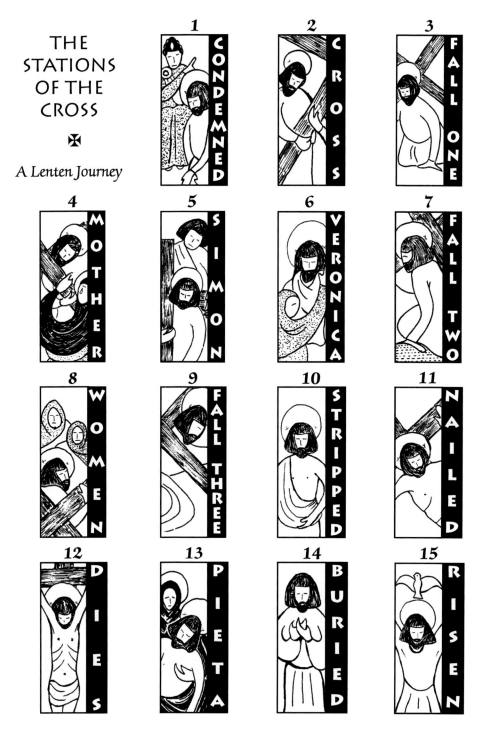

# PALM SUNDAY

*"Hosanna to the Son of David;*
*Blessed is he who comes in the name of the Lord"*

Holy Week begins on Palm Sunday – Jesus' joyful entry into Jerusalem to the tumultuous welcome of some of his followers and disciples. That evening, he and the apostles are invited to a meal at the house of Martha and Mary and their brother, Simon, whom we know better as Lazarus but *Lazarus* is an added name, we might even say a nickname. Simon Lazarus is how he was known.

We recall the story of the raising of Lazarus after four days in the tomb, the sorrow of Martha and Mary and their even telling Jesus he should have come when they sent him the message – then their brother would not have died. The Gospel says Jesus waited two days before going in response to that message – telling us that it is on the third day, the day of God's wonderful blessing which appears more than thirty times in the Scriptures, the Bible, that he goes to them.

The sisters' sadness in reproaching Jesus becomes Jesus' sadness. He weeps for his friend and then prays. God answers the prayer by allowing divinity to work through Jesus (Jesus was human, his divinity "as my Father gives me to speak and act") and Lazarus is brought to life. We easily imagine the welcome Jesus must have always received when he came to see the family. On the evening of Palm Sunday he is at their home in Bethany, a short distance from Jerusalem.

It was not a peaceful evening. There was blunt speaking, a loving action misunderstood, tensions of different understandings and relationships. Jesus tried to bring calm but we are aware of family and disciples not at ease.

In the evening of the day of the Resurrection, according to Luke, Jesus returns to Bethany with his apostles and disciples and from there ascends to his Father. He wanted Martha, Mary and Lazarus to share the wonder, the completion of the week of sorrow and glory? Martha and Mary see a different resurrection from that of their brother and Lazarus is aware of the difference between coming back to life and being raised from the dead.

Mark also speaks of Jesus' leaving them that evening, but from the Upper Room; and Luke gives an entirely different account at the beginning of the Acts of the Apostles when, forty days after the Resurrection, Jesus takes the disciples to the Mount of Olives to the Garden of Gethsemane. His agony and ascension are at the same place, his suffering transformed into glory, and from there he returns to the Father. How do we explain two such different accounts by Luke, in his Gospel and in the Acts?

Simply, said a fourteen-year-old girl in the classroom: Jesus ascended many times – Bethany was the first and the Mount of Olives was the last. In between he was instructing his disciples. These are not calendar days: 40 is a mystical number (years or days) symbolising God's eternity in human time. Holy Week begins and ends in Bethany.

## The Ascension

*"God goes up with shouts of joy*
*the Lord goes up with trumpet blast"*

*The image of heaven as 'above' and earth as 'below' is a simple one, used throughout the scriptures. It is a way of suggesting movement between God and us ("He came down", "He went up"). There is no actual movement – it happens within ("I'm in heaven", "I'm down in the doldrums").*

*The cloud that takes Jesus from his disciples is the scriptural image for the presence of God whom we cannot see. The divine Cloud leads the people to the Promised Land (the 'Pillar of Cloud'), Moses goes into the Cloud on Mount Sinai to receive the commandments, a voice speaks from the Cloud at Jesus' baptism and transfiguration and, so delicately at the Annunciation, Mary is told "the power of the most high will overshadow you".*

*St Augustine wrote of Jesus' incarnation and ascension that he did not leave the Father when he came to live with us, nor did he leave us when he returned to the Father: he is always, from eternity, with the Father; always one with us through his living presence. We know that beautiful truth in a fully human way: St John Chrysostom wrote*

*"Those whom we love and lose are no longer where they were before,*
*they are now with us wherever we go."*

# DATE OF THE LAST SUPPER

*"This is my Body which will be given up for you"*

Parents can be disturbed by what their children bring home from school, especially by what is being taught in the religion lessons. They may sometimes wonder if Catholic schools are building up or undermining the traditional faith so loved in the family.

One home in our parish was puzzled by a teasing question from their son. "When did Jesus have the Last Supper with his disciples?" They gave their obvious answer: on Maundy Thursday. He said it was two days before, on the Tuesday. They laughed, until he explained . . . .

Jesus went to the Garden of Gethsemane after the supper. It was dark, so was late. Soldiers with torches arrested him and took him to the house of Annas, father-in-law of Caiaphas the high priest. Then, Jesus was brought before the Sanhedrin and faced a trial in which many witnesses were called. He was found guilty and brought before Pontius Pilate to have the verdict confirmed. Pilate was reluctant to condemn him, and sent him on to Herod. Herod and his soldiers mocked and beat Jesus before sending him back to Pilate – who then confirmed the guilty verdict. Following his journey to Calvary, Jesus was crucified at nine o'clock on Friday morning, Mark tells us, and died at about three o'clock in the afternoon.

The family agreed their son had made a fair summary of the Gospel accounts.

Then came the challenge of his question. There was no time between late Thursday evening and nine o'clock Friday morning for all recorded to have happened. Furthermore, according to Jewish law, trials had to take place in the hours of daylight and, if a verdict of death were given, twenty-four hours had to elapse before the sentence could be carried out. There is no suggestion in the Gospel that the law was not complied with, and Pontius Pilate, as governor, would have made certain of this – we are told he did not want to condemn Jesus.

Having opened up the question the boy told the family that the Last Supper must have been on Tuesday evening, and Jesus was arrested then.

He went on trial before the Sanhedrin on the Wednesday and after the long trial ("many witnesses were called") was found guilty. On Thursday he came before Herod once and before Pontius Pilate twice and the guilty verdict was confirmed. Then, early on Friday morning (Mark says nine o'clock, *the third hour*), Jesus was crucified.

Why would Jesus have celebrated the Last Supper on Tuesday, the family asked: it wasn't the Passover. But it was, said the boy! Christian scholars have recently discovered that there were two calendars in use in the Holy Land in the time of Jesus, a lunar and a solar calendar. According to the solar calendar (of 364 days), the Passover was always celebrated on a Wednesday; but in the lunar calendar the 15th of Nisan (always the date of the Passover) might fall on any day. Jesus and his disciples must have followed the solar calendar, celebrating the Passover on Wednesday (beginning with the meal on Tuesday evening), whilst Jerusalem that year celebrated Passover on the Saturday.

The family were still doubtful, but their son showed them, in the Gospel according to Matthew and Mark, that Jesus had a meal at Bethany with Martha and Mary and their brother Simon Lazarus two days before the Passover: but John's Gospel says the meal was six days before the Passover. Both are right! They confirm two calendars - two different days on which the Passover was celebrated. Some people think that Jesus anticipated the Passover meal, knowing he would be dead on the Friday evening when the official Passover in Jerusalem was to be celebrated – but if Jesus did have the meal on Tuesday evening it was a true Passover meal according to the solar calendar.

I mentioned the discussion to a fellow priest, and he was angry. Our people don't want to be confused by raising such questions, he said. But a sure way to turn away people from the Church is to refuse to answer their questions, to be afraid of new knowledge and understanding. Jesus praised bringing *new and old* out of the treasure house and I was glad to know that such questions could be discussed at a Catholic school. Have we mistakenly been celebrating the Last Supper on Maundy Thursday?

# STANDING NEAR THE CROSS

*"Standing near the cross were his mother,
his mother's sister, Mary of Clopas and Mary of Magdala"*

(John 20:19)

"Standing near the Cross were his mother, his mother's sister, Mary of Clopas and Mary of Magdala." We know the verse so well. How many women are there, three or four?

If there are three, Mary of Clopas might be a cousin ('sister') of the mother of Jesus – so could have the same name. Three Marys standing near the cross.

But if there are four women, we realise that only two of them have been named – Mary Clopas and Mary Magdalen; the mother of Jesus and her sister are not named. Why are their first names not given? In her only other appearance in John (the Wedding at Cana) Mary is called "the mother of Jesus". We would not know her personal name if we only knew the Gospel according to John.

This is strange. No one would have known her better than John. At the Cross Jesus gave his mother into John's care. We assume they would have talked about the life and ministry they had shared with Jesus, the mystery of the Incarnation that they, above all, would have been able to meditate upon. We wonder why Mary appears only twice in John and why Jesus addresses her both times as "Woman". Why would John hide her name, and that of her sister?

Look at the Passion story in the other Gospel accounts. In Matthew Mary is not mentioned, but the other three women are: Mary Magdalen, Mary the mother of James and Joseph (she is Mary Clopas), and the mother of Zebedee's sons! So the sister of the mother of Jesus is Zebedee's wife and is the mother of James and John – two of the first four apostles to be called! James and John were Jesus' first cousins and in Mark we discover their mother's name was Salome.

There is a pattern. Jesus chose as his first apostles two of his cousins – along with their two friends, Simon and Andrew. Jesus began, as many would on any important mission, asking relatives and friends to help him.

Suddenly, Uncle Zebedee and cousins James and John in their fishing-boat becomes a family portrait.

Now a moment of the Gospel comes alive in a new way. We remember the mother of James and John approaching Jesus to ask for her sons to sit, one at his right hand and the other at his left, when he came into his kingdom, and we understand the anger of the other apostles who recognise family pressure for favour – a possible blight on any organisation. Aunt Salome was asking her nephew to favour his cousins, something any mother might do.

Salome was refused by Jesus, but is at the cross as a faithful follower, supporting her sister in the agony of watching Jesus die. We see in Salome a loving sister, faithful and courageous, bearing with Mary the sorrow of Jesus' death.

She was able to accept Jesus' refusal without resentment – wanting the best for her sons, but asking for it too blatantly and risking the resentment of others – and loving the truth in Jesus that her sons came to show her. "Jesus is not simply Aunt Mary's son, our cousin, your nephew. We have seen and we have believed" . . . and so did Salome. She witnessed the death on the cross, she came to the tomb on the day of resurrection.

Why does John's Gospel not personally name Salome? Possibly because John himself never did. No son uses his mother's name. She was not 'Salome' to John, she was 'Mother'. The mother of Jesus was 'Aunt Mary'. John calls Mary the "Mother of Jesus" in the two occasions she is present in his Gospel, and Jesus uses the wonderful name "Woman" – for whom the world had waited (Genesis 3:15).

Perhaps we have found why the Mary's and Salome's personal names are not given . . . John never used them, so neither did the disciples who wrote the Gospel in his name.

---

The letters JHS stand for *'Iesus (Jesus) Hominum Salvator'*, translated *'Jesus Saviour of Humanity'*.
The letters are a faulty Latin transliteration of the first three letters of the name Jesus in Greek (IHS) and the title is often written JHS as there was no 'J' in the original Latin.

# MARY OF CLOPAS

*"There were some women watching . . ."*

Mary of Clopas is involved in the sorrow and suffering at the crucifixion. She is named as one of the women and we are invited to understand more of why she was there.

The answer seems to lie in the name 'Clopas'. Clopas is the name of Mary's husband and is the name of one of the two disciples on the road to Emmaus on Easter Sunday afternoon – the wonderful story of resurrection excitement, incredulity, the breaking of bread and the recognising of the Lord, the racing back to Jerusalem to share the good news. Clopas is one of the two disciples – who is the other?

Clopas and his companion recognise Jesus in the Eucharistic moment: "he took bread, blessed it, broke it and gave it to them" (Luke 24:30). It is the Last Supper again, and they recognise him! But the Last Supper had been the only occasion at which Jesus had "taken, blessed, and broken bread": so they must have been there – to be able to recognise that moment at the inn near Emmaus.

We see the Paschal Meal in a new light: not simply the twelve apostles with the Lord but others of the disciples, too, sharing the great meal of the Jewish year. Families and friends together. We glimpse a wonderfully larger group than the twelve that the Gospel indicates and we see the mother of Jesus, as Pope John Paul II did, in a beautiful Maundy Thursday meditation.

He spoke of the wonder of the moment at the Last Supper when Mary received from Jesus his sacramental body and blood – she, who had given him his human body and blood. The human and the sacramental presence of Christ are manifest, and we share Mary's intimate involvement in both. "This is my body, received from you, given for you," we dare to imagine Jesus' thought. What wonderful love in a such a sacramental moment. Around the hushed gathering the disciples glimpse a mystery they do not yet understand, then each disciple receives a share in the Eucharistic mystery, Clopas and his companion amongst them – and on Easter Sunday they receive the same sacramental gift in the inn on the road to Emmaus.

Mary was the wife of Clopas and they would have been in Jerusalem for the Passover. They did not come for the death of Jesus. At this most sacred of family meals Mary and Clopas would have been together. Then she is at the Crucifixion. Where was her husband? Had he fled with the other disciples?

Mary of Clopas, at the Last Supper, the Crucifixion – was she even the other disciple on the road to Emmaus?

Look again at the story of the Crucifixion in Matthew and Mark; they say (as does John) that Mary was there – but they call her the "mother of James and Joset". This gives yet another thread to follow.

Four times the New Testament gives a list of the apostles (but notice the lists differ) – Acts 1:13, Luke 6:14, Matthew 10:2, Mark 3:16 – and each time the name "James, son of Alphaeus," occurs. Alphaeus is Clopas (Cleopas) – so James is also Mary's son! The question widens. James was important in the Jerusalem Christian community; he presided at the First Council of the Church in 49 AD, a letter under his name is in the New Testament, and he is several times referred to as the cousin of the Lord. Thus, his mother and his father are aunt and uncle to the Jesus!

Mary, wife of Clopas and mother of James, stood near the cross because she belonged to Jesus as family and as disciple. Alongside her were Salome, mother of James and John – two other of the apostles – and Mary, the mother of Jesus. The three women were related and Mary Magdalen belongs with them in an extraordinary picture of sadness and courage. Was Mary Magdalen at the Last Supper?

 Μαρια

The name *Mary* comes from the Latin and Greek name *Maria (Mariam and Mariamme)*, which was the single most popular name for about one in four Palestinian Jewish women of the Hebrew tribe of Levi during the time of Jesus. *Miriam* was the name of the sister of Moses and, like other Levite names, *Miriam* is thought to be Eqyptian in origin from the name Μαρια meaning 'beloved'.

# THE SHROUD AND HOLY SATURDAY NIGHT

*"Nicodemus brought one hundred pounds of spices and ointment for Jesus' burial . . ."*

We are told that Jesus died about three o'clock on (Good) Friday afternoon. A little while later his body was taken down from the cross, wrapped in a shroud and laid in the tomb. The women from Galilee were watching and went home to buy and prepare ointments and spices – intending to return after the Sabbath to give Jesus' body the proper burial according to Jewish custom. The Sabbath began at six o'clock on Friday evening and finished at six o'clock on the Saturday. Women from Galilee would not come in the hours of darkness, but would wait until light on Sunday morning. Mark (16:1) says they prepared on Saturday evening but Luke (23:56) says they prepared on the Friday evening.

Early on Sunday morning they came to the tomb, but there was no body. The Gospel accounts vary, but all suggest there was no body. Mary Magdalen came to tell Peter and John and they went running to the tomb. John reached the tomb first, saw the linen cloths that had been around the body, but did not go in. (Linen cloths! Where is the shroud?) Peter arrived and went into the tomb, John following him.

Now John saw the linen cloths and the headband more clearly and the headband – not with the cloths but wrapped up in a place by itself. Then come the wonderful words: "He saw and he believed" (John 20:8). What did he see inside the tomb that he did not see from outside – in the cloths and the headband, the *othnia* and the *sudarium*? And where is the shroud? Matthew, Mark and Luke all say that the body was left wrapped in a shroud. It has been taken away.

There is no shroud. Where is it? Someone must have been to the tomb before Sunday dawn, taken the shroud from the body and wrapped the body in its linen cloths. Who? When? It cannot be the women, because the reason for their coming to the tomb with spices and ointments is to give Jesus' body its burial. They know nothing of a full burial. Who was it?

Joseph of Arimathea. He brought down the body of Jesus from the cross, with the help of Nicodemus, and placed it in the tomb. Can you imagine their considering when they would come to give the blood-encrusted torn body the washing and anointing that Jewish piety demanded? It would be after the Sabbath – after six o'clock on the Saturday evening. They would be free, had authority over the soldiers, they were members of the Sanhedrin and the tomb belonged to Joseph. Did they go alone?

Standing at the cross were the mother of Jesus and John. The Gospel indicates John was friendly with members of the Sanhedrin, of which Joseph and Nicodemus were members. They would naturally have invited Mary and John to come.

We picture the four of them coming to the tomb on the Saturday evening. Lovingly and sadly they wash and anoint Jesus' body so that it may be given a proper burial. There is no awareness of the resurrection here. Carefully, they wrap the cloths around the body and finally the headband around the face and head. Their task completed, they withdraw from the tomb and the stone is put back in place.

On Sunday morning John is startled to learn from Mary Magdalen that the body has been taken away. He runs with Peter, and from outside the tomb he sees the cloths. He follows Peter into the tomb, sees the cloths close up – and believes! What has he seen? He has seen that the cloths are exactly as he and the others left them on the Saturday evening. The body has passed through them, leaving them wrapped as they had been – 'othnia' in the shape of the body and the 'sudarium' just as they had carefully bandaged it around Jesus' face and head. There has been a resurrection.

We return to reading the full Gospel account and we see that the details were there all the time. Joseph and Nicodemus brought one hundred pound of spices and ointment for Jesus' burial (John 19:39-40). It was they who gave Jesus' body its full burial, and the only time possible was on the Saturday night.

*"He saw and he believed"*
John 20:8

# THE FOUR RESURRECTION STORIES

*On the first day of the week . . .*
*as dawn was breaking* (Matthew) *. . . just after sunrise* (Mark) *. . .*
*very early in the morning* (Luke) *. . . while it was still dark* (John)

"I believe in the resurrection of Jesus from the dead . . ." – but can you tell the story? Matthew tells of two women who go to the tomb, whilst Mark and Luke tell of three – but not the same three – and John speaks of Mary Magdalen alone.

Matthew says the women went before dawn, Mark when the sun was rising, Luke at dawn and John when it was still dark. Mark and Luke say the women brought spices and ointments for Jesus' burial: Luke says they bought them on Friday evening, but Mark says on Saturday evening. Matthew tells of the women's seeing the angel roll back the stone from the tomb (terrifying the soldiers but reassuring the women not to be afraid); Mark says the stone was rolled away before the women reached the tomb and that the angel was waiting for them inside – although Luke says there were two angels waiting.

In John, Mary Magdalen goes to tell Peter and John about Jesus' body having been taken away, and the apostles race to see what has happened; but Luke says the apostles thought the women were talking nonsense. Mark has the angel tell the women to give a message for the apostles to meet Jesus in Galilee, but they were too frightened to go; yet Matthew says they were running to tell the apostles when they met Jesus – who gave them the same message the angel had given in Mark.

Nobody saw the Resurrection. The women and the apostles saw an empty tomb. They did see the cloths that had been around Jesus' body, though not the body itself.

Even though no one saw the Resurrection we have accounts of a number of people who saw the risen Lord – the women in the morning, Clopas and companion on the road to Emmaus in the afternoon, the disciples in the Upper Room that same evening – and appearances to Peter, James, and more than five hundred of the brethren that St Paul speaks about (1 Corinthians 15). If only we knew how they saw Jesus!

St Paul says that in our death our earthly body dies and in our resurrection our spiritual body rises (1 Corinthian 15:45-49). Do we express Jesus' death and resurrection in the same way? If so, how do we account for Jesus' wounds – and do we believe that our own disfigurements will be visible in the resurrection? Why were Mary Magdalen and Clopas slow to recognise Jesus?

There is one event – Jesus raised from the dead – and the Gospel traditions are independent witnesses to that event: they illustrate that people do not simply repeat what they hear, but interpret and then tell the story their own way. More, when people tell a story for the second time they choose new words; each telling of a story shaped by the listeners and the mood of the speaker.

God reveals truth in Jesus, the Word, but we vary the human words when we try to express that truth. The bibles we read have been translated. Comparisons show us how differently translators tell the same biblical event. No one can say with confidence "That is what it says and must mean", about the Bible: we have to ask "what does it mean?" and seek to understand. The original event, story, teaching was remembered and recorded differently, written by the evangelists, copied with mistakes and changes, translated by many with different understandings - so what we read is far from the original moment.

We may feel challenged by four accounts of the Resurrection that cannot be fitted together but the Church has never been concerned about the differences. We should be true to the Gospel and to the Church and tell the four accounts, not merge them into one inadequate summary. "Some women (woman) went to the tomb round about dawn . . ." How would we continue? Far better to accept the mystery within four different tellings – and not summarise them into one story.

### *"Noli mi tangere"*
*To Mary Magdalene Jesus said*
*"Do not hold on to me, I am ascending to my Father"* (John 20:17)

*Jesus greeted them. The women knelt before him,*
*clasping his feet "Do not be afraid," he said.* (Matthew 28:9-10)

# GOSPEL MOMENTS: THE BREAKING OF BREAD

*"I have been longing to eat the passover with you before my suffering . . ."*
*then he took bread, blessed and broke it and gave it to them*

On the afternoon of the day of Jesus' resurrection two of his disciples were on the road to Emmaus, about seven miles from Jerusalem. As they walked they were talking about the events in Jerusalem during the recent few days. Jesus joined them in their walk and asked what they were discussing. They did not recognise this stranger and were surprised he did not know about the Jerusalem events. They told him their story – ending with the extraordinary possibility that Jesus had risen from the dead. They were looking at Jesus, speaking with him, but they did not recognise him.

Jesus opens the Scriptures to them, showing how many passages looked forward to these recent events, prophesying his suffering and death – and the disciples' hearts are touched. When they reach an inn, they persuade him to stay with them. They sit for a meal. Jesus takes bread, blesses it, breaks it and gives it to them – and their eyes are opened. They recognise him as Jesus – he is now the risen Christ!

They recognise him at the breaking of bread – but he had broken bread only once before, at the Last Supper. They must have been present at the Last Supper to recognise this moment and its significance. Clopas and his companion were at the Last Supper? Wonderful possibility.

Clopas. We already know his name. Mary of Clopas (his wife) stood alongside the mother of Jesus at Calvary – one of the three (or four) women standing near the cross. Clopas and Mary were in Jerusalem for the great feast of the Passover and it would have been natural for relations and friends to gather for the greatest family meal of the Jewish year.

We picture Clopas and Mary with their two apostle sons, Matthew (Levi) and James, together with a whole community from Galilee at the Passover meal that became the Last Supper, and the celebration of the Eucharist to the first Christian community in the breaking of bread.

Artists do not picture such a large gathering, but the Gospel and prayerful meditation allow us to imagine that gathering and, with Pope John Paul II, to focus on one person, the mother of Jesus, and a beautiful moment.

"Mother, you gave me who I am and I give you whom I have become – your son offering himself to our heavenly Father as the bread broken for many."

We follow Pope John Paul and picture the sharing of the Eucharist to all who were present, Clopas and Mary amongst them. At Emmaus, a few days later, Clopas and his companion receive the Eucharist once more and recognise the risen Christ has been their companion along the road.

*Jesus said "What are you talking about so seriously?"*
*They stopped.*
*"Have you not heard what has happened these last few days?*
*Jesus the Nazarene was condemned to die and was crucified -*
*but some of our friends say he has come back to life!"*
*Jesus explained to them what Moses, the prophets,*
*the scriptures said about him.*

# THE TWELVE, OR SO, APOSTLES

*Only seven of the apostles are named
as being present at the Last Supper.
Do we presume all the apostles were there?*

After Jesus' Ascension on the Mount of Olives the apostles went back to the Upper Room where they were staying, says Luke at the opening of the Acts of the Apostles (Acts 1:13-14). He gives the names of the apostles, and they are familiar.

Familiar names are missing. We go looking for other lists of the apostles and find them in Matthew (10:1-4), Mark (3:13-19) and Luke (6:12-16) – all are different! We cannot name the twelve apostles: we can only name twelve with some names left over . . .

A teacher friend tried it in class. Name the twelve apostles, he said. The most frequent start was "Matthew, Mark, Luke and John . . ." You will chuckle, knowing that there are only two apostles in that list of four – but how many apostles can you name with confidence?

There are two Simons, two James and two Judes. There are two sets of brothers, and possibly three. It is certain that some of the apostles are known by more than one name: Simon Peter Cephas Barjonah has four and Zebedee and Clopas Alphaeus have minor starring roles as the fathers of brothers chosen to be apostles.

Zebedee's sons are John and James, who are also called Sons of Thunder ('Boanerges') and his wife was the sister of Mary, the mother of Jesus. Her name was Salome. (In a dramatic reading of the Passion, by an unprepared reader, we heard that Salami was at the Crucifixion!)

Alphaeus' one son was James and his other son was named Levi. Mark and Luke tell us of Levi, sitting at the customs house, being called to follow Jesus, and Mark tells us that Levi is the son of Alphaeus. But Matthew tells the same story and names the new apostle as Matthew. The sons of Alphaeus are James and Levi Matthew.

The memory stirs. James became head of the Church at Jerusalem. He is called the brother (cousin) of the Lord. Thus Alphaeus must be Jesus' uncle – and Matthew-Levi will be Jesus' cousin! The story explodes.

Matthew was not a stranger at the customs house – he was Jesus' cousin, a traitor, a tax-collector hated by the people, a shame to his family. We can imagine the sad approach of Uncle Alphaeus to his nephew, Jesus: "My son, your cousin – will you win him back to us?" Jesus goes to the black sheep of the family at the customs' house and invites him to follow him.

Matthew and James, John and James – four cousins of the Lord! Now we look more closely at the names of the other apostles, and a new understanding begins to dawn. They were not strangers, they were all family and friends . . . of course! Just as we would do – Jesus seems to have invited those whom he knew and loved to come with him as his first disciples.

## The Evangelists

*The apostles did not write the Gospel accounts.*
*The writers of the Gospel (the Evangelists) did their own research within the early Christian communities. The Church chose the four accounts we know from a number and those other 'gospels' are worth reading.*
*In Christian art we find the Evangelists depicted by symbols.*

(The Angel) **Matthew** *was written about 75-80. Some scholars suggest there was an early account written in the language that Jesus spoke, Aramaic. There is no trace of such a document. We do not know if 'Matthew' is the apostle.*

(The Lion) **Mark** *was written in Rome round about the year 60. It is clear that Mark reflects a great deal of what St Peter told him and was, we believe, the boy in Mark 14:51-52.*

(The Ox) **Luke** *was written about 75-80, based upon documents he found in researching within those first Christian communities. However, the first two chapters were not written by him but are included as given to him. We wonder by whom . . .*

(The Eagle) **John** *was written by his own disciples, probably in the early 2nd century. They call him "the disciple Jesus loved". John was the last of the books of the Bible to be written.*

# LIKE THAT?

*The soldiers twisted thorns and made for him a crown.*
*They spat at him, struck him, made fun of him.*
*They blindfolded him and, finally,*
*crucified him.*

Why did Jesus have to die like that? The question was asked by a ten-year-old girl. I loved the question. She had no problem with Jesus dying – it was his suffering death that hurt her. She had come to love him in what family and school had taught her about him, and she thought everyone should have loved him. But people hated him and crucified him. Why couldn't he have grown old and died peacefully?

I brought the question to the people at our parish discussion group. It's encouraging to think of parishes around the country meeting to explore with love and reverence our wonderful faith. Mind and heart God has given us, and it is good to know of churches at prayer and in discussion. How do we grow in love and understanding unless we see the truth, grow in faith?

I was told what I should have told her. *Only by dying as he did could Jesus have earned our salvation.* That made God sound like a blood-thirsty ogre rather than a loving Father, said someone. *Only a perfect death could take away sin.* No, God's loving forgiveness could take away any sin - we do it for each other all the time. *Only by suffering could Jesus show his love for us.* But we don't suffer to prove our love for each other - we simply show love, as did Jesus before ever he suffered.

*Jesus was the new lamb of sacrifice: the Old Testament Paschal Lamb was a sign of God's freeing his people from slavery, and Jesus is the Lamb of God who redeems us from the slavery of sin.* Good balance, but it suggests an offended God asking for a death in sacrifice. Jesus did not speak about his Father like that.

Then, enter Duns Scotus, our own Scottish Franciscan, who taught a beautiful doctrine. We follow his central thought: Jesus was always going to come as the supreme sign of God's love. Jesus did not come in order to save us, but as the wonderful climax of Creation.

Duns Scotus could not accept that sin changed God's original plan, causing a saviour to be sent, because that would make evil seem stronger than good. He taught that Creation reached the pinnacle of perfection at the Incarnation. In Jesus, the human and divine are one, time and eternity touch and the finite and the infinite are brought together. Jesus' incarnation is the climax, the perfection of Creation. In John (10:10) Jesus cries out "I came that they might have life and have it to the full." Wonderful words. Through Jesus we are offered forgiveness in the fullness of life.

Jesus was always coming to bring that fullness, said Scotus. When he came the power of sin wrestled with him and crucified him – then, in his resurrection the fullness of life is given! The little girl smiled when I reported back from our group.

*Save us, Saviour of the World*

*for by your Cross*

*and Resurrection*

*you have set us free*

# WOOD'S SECRETS

*"Behold, because of the wood of a tree,
Joy has come into the world"*

I am the past, the present and the future;
    the rings I wear tell the years.
First, I bore knowledge, taken too soon and misused.
    I brought people to salvation,
        carrying them on and through the waters,
            and leading them across the lands.
It was I that cradled the infant and, as he grew,
    he worked and shaped me for use by his people.
Then, in love of all people
    he carried me and I held him,
        suffering in death,
            as the world tried to destroy his truth.
As does his truth, I shall continue
    giving life and shelter and hope to all creation,
        offering knowledge,
            a knowledge that requires patience,
                for my strength and being are obvious,
                    and can be clearly seen;
    but you will need to look more closely
        to discover my uniqueness.
In my roots you must believe, as I can only promise
    that they are because I am.
        I am the Tree of Life:
            your future, your present and your past.

© Watermead "Verba" Collection 18

# HOLY WEEK AND EASTER
# TELLING THE STORY

Can you tell the story of Easter morning? There are four different times given in the four Gospel accounts. Which one would you choose in your story? How many women went to the tomb? John says one, Matthew two, Mark three and Luke three – but not the same three. How many women in your version of the story?

The details don't matter, you may say: what matters is that I believe in the resurrection. Agreed. But would you allow a Catholic teacher to say that, or a Catholic priest or deacon? What sort of teachers or preachers would they be if their attitude was "Who cares, as long as we believe." Poor students, poor people, with teachers and preachers like that. They have studied to be able to teach and preach. How well did they study if they have no answers to questions as straightforward as what time was it? How many women were there?

How about the angels. They are in each account – one in Matthew and Mark, but two in Luke and John. Would you remember that in your telling the story of Easter morning? What do we really know of what we say we believe? We can't share our belief if we know nothing. Time, women, angels – how is your version of the Easter story shaping up?

In one account the women meet Jesus. Which one? In Luke, where Peter believes the women's message and goes to the tomb alone, he looks in and sees the cloths. Cloths? Surely there was a shroud? Luke and Matthew and Mark all say that Jesus' body was wrapped in a shroud late on the Friday afternoon. Where has it gone? Who took it and when?

Look at John's account and be even more puzzled. Here, Peter and the other disciple go running to the tomb, the other disciple running faster than Peter and reaching the tomb first, sees the cloths but does not go into the tomb. Peter arrives, goes straight into the tomb and sees the cloths, especially the one that had been around Jesus' head rolled up in a place by itself. Then the other disciple enters and sees the cloths close up. "He saw and he believed." What did he see close up that he had not seen from outside the tomb?

The cloths were undisturbed, still in the shape of the body they had enwrapped, and the headband in its place around the head. They had not been unwound! They were still as wrapped around Jesus' body and head, but the body was not there and no one had unwrapped the cloths – Jesus had passed through them, leaving them undisturbed!

Impossible! No, resurrection. Work out what happened.

Joseph and Nicodemus took Jesus' body down from the cross late on Friday afternoon. There was no time for the full burial rights, so they planned to return when the sabbath was over, on the Saturday evening, and give the cleansing and anointing that there was no time for on the Friday.

Did they come alone? Of course not. They invited the mother of Jesus to come with them. It belonged to her love to perform that final duty. With her came the beloved disciple into whose care Jesus had given her: "Behold your son" and "the disciple took her to himself."

Picture the four of them on that Saturday evening. It is Joseph's own tomb and he and Nicodemus, as members of the Sanhedrin, had authority over the soldiers. They wash and anoint the body, take away the bloodied shroud and wrap the winding cloths (othnia) around Jesus' body, and the last one, the one which went around his head (the sudarium). Late on Saturday night they finish their task and go home. And there it is written in John's gospel: Nicodemus brought one hundred pounds of spices and ointments for the burial.

Early the following morning Mary Magdalene tells the apostles that Jesus' body has gone. Peter and the other disciple run to the tomb. The disciple follows Peter into the tomb and the cloths are as he and the others left them the previous night, but there is no body. The body had passed through the cloths. Resurrection. That is the story. How would you tell it?

*"He saw and he believed"*
John 20:8

In school, at the beginning of every Year 11 (Form 5), I asked the youngsters to read the four accounts of the resurrection and make a summary. In a few moments they saw the impossibility. Have you ever given a few minutes to read the four accounts?

The Passover Meal, the Last Supper, was held in the evening, the beginning of the Jewish day. After their meal, Jesus and the disciples went to the Garden of Gethsemane on the Mount of Olives. There he was arrested. On Friday morning he was crucified at the third hour (9 am) we learn from Mark's Gospel.

Jesus at the houses of Annas and Caiaphas, in court before the Sanhedrin ("and many witnesses were called"), at the palace of Pontius Pilate, the court of King Herod, scourged and crowned with thorns – between late Thursday evening and early Friday morning? Surely impossible.

By law, a trial had to take place in the hours of daylight. There is no hint in the Gospel that due process was not followed. A verdict of the death sentence required a waiting period of twenty-four hours during which new evidence might be brought to mitigate the sentence. Pontius Pilate would never have allowed the process of law not to be observed, nor would members of the Sanhedrin, especially members like Joseph of Arimathea and Nicodemus.

Thursday as the evening of the Last Supper seems not possible. There is too little time for all that happens between the arrest and the crucifixion. So, when was it, and was it actually a Passover Meal?

Tuesday looks to be a good answer. The Passover is celebrated, and Jesus becomes the new Passover in the wonder of the Eucharist, bread and wine: "This is my body, this is my blood." After the meal they go to the Garden of Gethsemane where Jesus is arrested and taken to the house of Annas and, later or early morning, to the house of Caiaphas. (Research the relationship and relative powers of Annas and Caiaphas – you will be fascinated.)

On Wednesday, Jesus is brought before the court, the Sanhedrin. Many witnesses are called. At the end of the trial he is declared guilty and condemned to die. Now twenty-four hours must pass before sentence can be carried out.

On Thursday, Jesus appears before Pilate, then Herod, and returns to Pilate where sentence of death is confirmed. Early on Friday morning he is crucified at the third hour (9 o'clock) and dies at the ninth hour (3 o'clock in the afternoon).

His body is wrapped in a shroud and placed in Joseph's new tomb. All go home to celebrate the Sabbath and the Passover. When the Passover ends at 6 o'clock on the Saturday evening, Joseph and Nicodemus (bringing one hundred pounds of spices and ointments, says John's Gospel) come with Mary and the beloved disciple to wash and anoint Jesus' body, the full burial rights. Their loving task completed late that Saturday night, they go home.

On the Sunday morning there is no body. There are cloths, still unwound. There has been resurrection.

That the Passover was on Tuesday seems probable. An actual Passover or an anticipated one? The Gospel makes clear that Jerusalem celebrated the Passover on the Friday evening and Saturday, following the lunar calendar which was in general use in the Holy Land, but Jesus and the disciples seem to have been following the solar calendar.

In the solar calendar the Passover is celebrated on the 15th day Nisan (first month of the Jewish year) and the 15th Nisan is always a Wednesday and thus the Passover meal would have been on the Tuesday evening.

Following the lunar calendar, however, the 15th Nisan might be any day of the week (like our Christmas Day) and in the year of Jesus' death and resurrection the Passover was on the Saturday and the sacred meal on the Friday evening.

We have known about the two calendars since early in the 20th century when the solar calendar was rediscovered during research into the life of the Qumran Community. We had lost sight of it for centuries but now understand there were two calendars, solar and lunar, in use in Jesus' time, 15th Nisan always a Wednesday in the solar, but any day in the lunar. Jesus celebrated a true Passover Meal.

In the early Church there were severe disputes about the date to celebrate Easter. In the background we see two traditions of the Jewish Passover, following the lunar and the solar calendars.

# Christ's Farewell
## The Words

I shall go to my Father's house,
and prepare there a place for you.
I'll return to take you with me.
*Remember . . .*
*I am the Way, the Truth and the Life.*

I shall not leave you orphans,
I'll come back, take you with me.
As I live, so you shall live.
*Remember . . .*
*I am the Way, the Truth and the Life.*

If you love, you will keep my word,
and my Father will love you.
We shall come to dwell with you.
*Remember . . .*
*I am the Way, the Truth and the Life.*

Gift of peace I bequeath to you,
my own peace I now give to you,
peace the world knows not to give.
*Remember . . .*
*I am the Way, the Truth and the Life.*

We shall live, we shall dwell with you.
From this life we shall come to you:
you with us and we with you,
*Rememb'ring . . .*
*You are the Way, the Truth and the Life.*

Copyright © 1993 : Watermead Music Collection 1
Watermead hymn : Lyrics by John Daley IC

# Christ's Farewell
*The Music*

## A seasonal Watermead hymn to share with wording taken from Jesus' discourse at the Last Supper.

*Lyrics by John Daley IC*  *Music by Alison Kennedy*

"Christ's Farewell" Music Copyright 1993 © Watermead Music Collection 1

All our sheet music is copyrighted © Watermead Music, Watermead Publishing Ltd.
Permission granted to copy and use within a liturgical celebration only.
WATERMEAD MUSIC is part of the WATERMEAD APOSTOLATE..
For further queries or permission to use this music (other than as part of a liturgical celebration),
please contact us via our website (www.watermead-apostolate.co.uk)
or phone 0116 2207881 (+44 116 220 7881).

**SUGGESTED PERFORMANCE**

Instrumental parts are not provided as part of this presentation, as the hymn was originally written as a solo/choir meditation.

The suggestion is to use soloists and small choir groupings for the singing of the various verses with the full choir joining in at the singing of each refrain.

*(Note the wording of the final refrain is different from the previous four verses.)*

# A GOSPEL QUIZ

*A good question may surprise us to discover we do not know what we thought we knew. In this quiz No.10 is the impossible question - yet it looks the easiest. All the other questions require careful reading but the answers become clear. No.10 doesn't have an answer.*
(The answers to the following questions are on page 30)

**1.** Jesus' body was wrapped in a shroud on the Friday but when the disciples came to the tomb on the Sunday there were linen cloths and a headband. Who took the shroud and when?

**2.** Nathanael is one of the apostles and is mentioned twice in the Gospel, both in John. What was he doing on those two occasions?

**3.** Jesus was arrested after the Last Supper. He was crucified about 9.00 am (the third hour) on the Friday morning. Between his arrest and crucifixion he had a long trial before the Sanhedrin ("many witnesses were called"), was brought twice before Pontius Pilate and once before Herod. What night was he arrested?

**4.** We have three accounts of the calling of a disciple at the Customs house. (a) He has two names – what are they? (b) What was his father's name?

**5.** Another of the disciples has the same father as the disciple in question 4. What was the father's relationship to Jesus?

**6.** At the wedding feast of Cana water became wine, stone became flesh, six became seven. Please explain.

**7.** John says that Jesus had a meal at Bethany with Martha and Mary and their brother six days before the Passover. Mark says two days before the Passover. Is one of them mistaken? If both are right – how?

**8.** Are the centurion's servant (Matthew 8:5-13, Luke 7:1-10) and the nobleman's son (John 4:43-54) two versions of the same story or two different events? Did the centurion and Jesus actually meet each other?

**9.** The Law ordained (a) trials should take place during the hours of daylight; (b) if a verdict of death were passed a day should elapse before the sentence be carried out. Write a convincing timetable of Jesus' arrest, trial, condemnation and execution – allowing that the process of law was followed. Pontius Pilate and fair-minded members of the Sanhedrin would not have allowed the law to be by-passed.

**10.** Name the twelve apostles. Which of them were Jesus' cousins?

**11.** "Standing near the cross were his mother, his mother's sister, Mary of Clopas and Mary of Magdala." Are there three women or four? If there are four, what is the name of the sister?

**12.** Did Judas receive the Eucharist before he left the Last Supper?

**13.** How many women came to the tomb on the day of Resurrection? Name them.

**14.** Two of the Gospel accounts say that the thieves crucified with Jesus joined in mocking him and one Gospel account speaks of the good thief who defended him. Which are the Gospels and who is correct?

**15.** Name the brother of Martha and Mary. Lazarus is his nickname.

**16.** There are six Gospel accounts of the feeding of a large crowd. How many people were fed and how many loaves and fishes are there in the different accounts?

**17.** Jesus' genealogy (family line) is given by Matthew and Luke. Some of the details differ strangely. The greatest difference is that Matthew mentions four women. Who are they?

**18.** There is no stable in the Gospel stories of Jesus' birth. What places are mentioned by Matthew and Luke? Who are the people with Mary and Joseph who are astounded by what the shepherds tell them?

**19.** How many accounts of the Ascension are there? From where did the Ascension take place?

# GOSPEL QUIZ ANSWERS

1. Joseph, Nicodemus, John and Mary. Saturday evening.
2. (a) sitting under a fig tree; (b) fishing.
3. Tuesday.
4. (a) Levi, Matthew; (b) Clopas.
5. Uncle.
6. The water is for purification, symbolising Old Testament Law: the wine is the Eucharist, New Testament Law of love. The stone of the Old Testament Law becomes the flesh of Christ ("The Word was made flesh"). Six water jars become seven (Jesus is the seventh) vessels of the Eucharistic wine, the blood of Christ.
7. There were two calendars, Lunar and Solar, in use in the Holy Land, thus two Passover meals in that same week – Tuesday and Friday.
8. Probably the same story. In one of the three accounts Jesus and the centurion do not meet.
9. Tuesday – arrest; Wednesday – trial before the Sanhedrin; Thursday – before Pilate and Herod; Friday – Crucifixion.
10. This is the almost impossible question. We have too many names, and always some left over from any twelve we name.
11. Four women. Salome is the sister.
12. Almost certainly, yes.
13. The four Gospel accounts give different numbers. Even Mark and Luke, who name three, do not name the same three.
14. Matthew and Mark say the two thieves joined in the mockery, Luke speaks of the good thief. It is probable that Luke is correct. Artistic convention shows Jesus' head inclined to the right, towards the good thief. You will rarely see Jesus' head inclined to the left.
15. Simon.
16. 5,000; 5,000 not counting the women and children; 4,000; 4,000 not counting the women and children. Five loaves and two fish, seven loaves and a few fish.
17. Tamar, Rahab, Ruth, the wife of Uriah (Bathsheba).
18. Matthew refers to a house or dwelling place: Luke mentions no particular place but the Holy Family are surrounded by those to whom the shepherds tell their story.
19. Three different accounts in Mark, Luke, Acts. In Mark the Ascension took place from the Upper Room; in Luke from Bethany, a short distance from Jerusalem; in Acts, from the Mount of Olives, the Garden of Gethsemane.

# Watermead

Watermead is the name given to a Christian apostolate that shares faith through people's gifts, talents and time, recording and publishing our own music, cards, stationery, resources and books. We began in 1992, and over the years the apostolate has grown into one that has various aspects to its sharing - music, books, resources, greeting cards, stationery, evening and day retreats, pilgrimages.

Everything we produce is available from our Watermead shops (for more information see www.watermead-apostolate.co.uk).

## So many ways to share faith

Watermead began with music, sharing the original music being composed in the then parish community. As the music flowed it started to inspire the creativity in others and soon words, paintings and drawings were being donated to our Watermead projects.

Our first book was 'Words of Prayer and Encouragement' (1993) soon followed by 'Tom, an English-Irishman' (1994).

There have been various ways we have used the words given over the years - a daily prayer book and numerous greeting cards, with some prayers set to music by our apostolate composers.

The hymn given on page 25, 'Christ's Farewell', is amongst the first composed, second with Fr John as lyricist, and immediately booked by several members of our original apostolate choir for their funeral. Sadly those requests have since been fulfilled, although their voices are preserved through their singing for our first cassette recording 'Our Songs Give praise' - their musical gift continuing to be shared.

## Retreats

Throughout his priesthood Fr John has led retreats, opening up the scriptures to those who come, bringing them alive and relevant to today's world and its challenges. In 1994 he started to share the instrumental versions of our hymns at these retreats as prayerful reflections to conclude the sessions, sharing the individual stories that inspired each hymn - 'Music as Prayer' the title used.